The BRILLIANT BOOK OF EASY CRAFTS

The BRILLIANT BOOK OF EASY CRAFTS

Anna-Marie D'Cruz and Rita Storey

WAYLAND

Published in paperback in 2014
by Wayland
Copyright © Wayland 2014

Wayland
338 Euston Road
London NW1 3BH

Wayland
Level 17/207 Kent Street
Sydney NSW 2000

Senior editor: Jennifer Schofield
   and Victoria Brooker
Designer: Jane Hawkins and Basement68

The author and publisher would like
to thank the following models: Husnen
Ahmad, Emel Augustin, Hannah Barton,
Jade Campbell, Ammar Duffus, Teya
Hutchison, Akash Kohli, Ellie Lawrence,
Adam Menditta, Eloise Ramplin, Robin
Stevens and Toby Whitehouse.

Picture Credits:
All photography by Chris Fairclough
except 13 Archivo Iconografica, S.A./
CORBIS; 17 top Dallas and John Heaton/
Free Agents Limited/CORBIS; 41 Richard
Cummins/CORBIS; 57 Getty Images 2007;
85 bottom right Pete Saloutos/CORBIS;
105 top Popperfoto/Getty Images; 109
Time & Life Pictures/Getty Images.

Some of the material in this book
appeared in the 'Make and Use'
series, also published by Wayland.

British Library Cataloguing in Publication
Data
   The children's book of easy crafts.
   1. Handicraft--Juvenile literature.
   I. Title II. Easy crafts
   745.5-dc23

ISBN: 978 0 7502 8337 3
Printed in China

10 9 8 7 6 5 4 3 2 1

Wayland is a division of
Hachette Children's Books,
an Hachette UK company.
www.hachette.co.uk

The crafts in this book are designed
to be made by children. However, we
recommend adult supervision at all
times as the publisher cannot be held
responsible for any injury caused while
making these projects.

Contents

Before you begin

These easy-to-follow, step-by-step instructions will show you how to make some fantastic crafts. You can adapt these projects, too, using different colours and materials. Let your imagination run wild!

Preparation

Before you can start making your crafts, you need to prepare. Check you have everything listed in the 'You will need' panel for each project. If the projects need paint or glue, cover any surfaces with newspaper so it's easy to clean up any spills. Put on an apron or wear an old top. Find a space where you can leave your projects to dry at the end.

Craft materials

You'll find that most projects need the following:

Glue - PVA glue is great for mixing into paint to make it stronger. Glue sticks are useful for sticking smaller items. Glitter glues could be used to add a bit of extra sparkle.

Paintbrushes - Have a few different-sized paintbrushes handy. Use smaller ones for drawing fine lines or features and thicker paintbrushes for colouring in bigger areas.

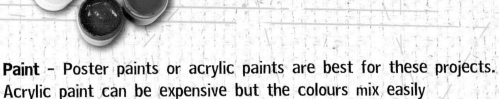

Paint – Poster paints or acrylic paints are best for these projects. Acrylic paint can be expensive but the colours mix easily and dry quickly. Poster paints are easy to wash off.

Paper and card – It's always good to have a selection of different coloured card and paper handy so that you can easily start a craft project. Crepe paper and tracing paper are handy to have, too.

Recycling

Remember that you can reuse cardboard, paper, cardboard tubes and drinks bottles for some of these crafts so keep a store of them if you have space. Why not collect buttons, sequins, scraps of fabric and ribbons to decorate your crafts?

Cleaning up afterwards

It's not fun, but it has to be done! Make sure you wash up all of your paint and glue brushes or they will go hard. Wipe down any surfaces to remove any paint, glue or glitter. Put lids back on glues, paints and glitter sticks so that they don't dry out. Tidy everything away. Then you're ready for when you next want to craft!

Be careful!

• Wear an apron or old top to keep clean.

• Close scissors when they're not being used. Carry them with the point facing down to your toes. Don't leave them near table edges or in places where younger siblings or pets can reach them.

• Keep kitchen roll or old rags nearby to clean up spills or splashes.

• Check that all paints and glues are safe for children and non-toxic.

• Wash your hands well with soap and water after you've finished.

8

Masks

Contents

All about masks

A mask is something that covers all or part of the face to hide it or to change its appearance. Masks have decorated faces throughout history — from Stone Age huntsmen, Egyptian mummies and Greek actors to today's modern performers.

Masks from long ago

Masks were used as far back as the Stone Age when huntsmen are believed to have disguised themselves as animals before stalking their prey. In Ancient Egypt, funerary masks were used to cover the face of a mummy so that the dead person's soul would recognise the person's body in the afterlife. Some of these masks have been found in Egyptian tombs, such as King Tutankhamun's mask (see right).

Theatre costumes

Actors in Ancient Greek and Roman theatres used masks to show emotion (feeling). In Greek theatre, all the characters were played by men, so those playing women wore masks of female characters. In Italian comedy theatre, commedia dell'arte, the lively characters were portrayed with the help of silly-looking masks. In Japanese Noh theatre, the actors create the characters through body movement and masks. Today, television and film actors sometimes wear masks as part of the special effects that help make the characters more believable.

Get started

In this book you can discover ways of making interesting masks from around the world. Try to use materials that you already have either at home or at school. For example, for the cardboard in these projects, the backs of used-up notepads, art pads and hardbacked envelopes are ideal. Reusing and recycling materials like this is good for the environment and it will save you money. The projects have all been made and decorated for this book but do not worry if yours look a little different — just have fun making and wearing your masks. You could have a different face for each day of the week!

Aztec skull

You will need

- cream and white card · pencil
- pair of scissors · glue
- coloured pencils · wool · sticking tape
- hole punch · elastic cord

The Day of the Dead is an Aztec celebration that is still popular in Brazil and Mexico. The Aztecs believed that death is the beginning of a new stage of life, so the Day of the Dead is a happy time to celebrate people's lives on Earth. The skull is a popular symbol of this festival. Follow the steps to make your own skull mask.

1. Draw the shape shown onto cream card so that it is big enough to cover your face. Cut it out.

2. Use the information in the panel on the right to draw and cut out circles for the eyes. Make them large enough for you to see through. Similarly, cut out a triangular shape for your nose.

Making eyes!

1. Close your eyes. Use the hand that you do not use to write to point to your eyes.
2. Move your fingers onto the mask.
3. Use a pencil to mark where your fingers are and to draw eyes.
4. Cut out the eyes.

14

3. Draw and cut out teeth from the white card. Glue them onto the mask to make a mouth.

4. Use coloured pencils to cross-hatch parts of the mask to decorate it.

5. For the hair, cut lengths of wool and tape them to the top of the mask at the back so that they fall over the top of the mask.

6. To wear the mask, use a hole punch to make a hole on either side of the mask. Cut a cord of elastic that fits around your head, then thread it through the holes and tie it with a knot at each hole to keep it in place. Your mask is now ready to wear.

Khon mask

You will need
- A3 sheet of coloured card · pencil
- pair of scissors · newspaper
- paints · paintbrushes · glue
- glitter · sequins · foil stars
- gold pen · hole punch · elastic cord

Khon is a style of theatre performed in Thailand where the actors wear masks or crowns to represent animals, demons and gods. The masks are brightly coloured and often have gold crowns that are decorated with jewels. Use coloured paints and lots of glitter to decorate your mask.

1. Copy the shape shown onto the card, making it big enough to cover your face. Cut it out.

2. Follow the guide on page 14 to mark where the eyes need to be. Cut them out.

3. Use a pencil to draw on a design for the face.

16

4. Cover your work surface with newspaper. Use different coloured paints and a gold pen to decorate the face part of the mask. Leave the paint to dry.

5. To decorate the crown, cover a small section of it with glue and sprinkle it with glitter. When the glue has dried, cover the next section with glue, adding more glitter, sequins and foil stars.

6. When the glue has dried, the mask is ready to try on. Use a hole punch to make a hole on either side of the mask. Cut a cord of elastic that fits around your head, then thread it through the holes and tie it with a knot at each side to keep it in place.

Carnival jester

Masks are made for carnivals around the world. The most famous carnivals take place in Venice, Italy, Rio de Janeiro, Brazil and New Orleans, USA. The jester is one of the most popular carnival masks. Follow the steps to make your own.

1. Draw and cut out the shape shown from the card. Check that it fits across your face and over your nose, but does not cover your mouth. Cut out holes for your eyes, as shown on page 14.

2. Cut out shapes from the coloured paper to decorate the hat part of the mask. Staple rik rak round the edge of the eye part of the mask.

Mardi Gras

The New Orleans Mardi Gras (which means Fat Tuesday in French), is a time of parades and masked balls. The Mardi Gras lasts for a few weeks but it ends on Shrove Tuesday — the day before Lent starts.

3. To make the nose, fold a piece of card in half. Draw a triangle onto the card that is wide enough at one end to fit onto the nose of the mask. Cut out the nose.

4. Make a small cut, about 1cm long, along the fold at the widest end of the triangle.

5. Fold each side of the small cut upwards to make tabs.

6. Put double-sided tape onto each tab to stick the nose to the mask.

7. Use a hole punch to make a hole on either side of the mask. Cut a cord of elastic that fits around your head, then thread it through the holes and tie it with a knot at each side to keep it in place. Put on the mask and get into the carnival spirit.

19

Bwa Sun mask

You will need
- thin corrugated cardboard · pencil
- plate · pair of scissors · masking tape
- newspaper · PVA glue · string
- paints · paintbrushes · large lollipop stick

Crops need rain and sunshine to grow. In many countries, people depend on the rain and sunshine for all their food. This mask is worn by people in Burkina Faso in dance ceremonies to celebrate the farming season.

1. Draw around a plate onto the cardboard. Make sure the circle is large enough to cover your face. Cut it out. Use the guide on page 14 to cut out holes for the eyes.

2. To make the nose, cut a triangle of card and bend it down the middle. Put strips of masking tape down each side to stick it to the mask.

3. Spread glue around one of the eyeholes. Circle string around the eye hole until you have gone around four or five times. Do the same with the other eye hole.

4. To make a mouth, cut two circles from spare cardboard, one smaller than the other. Glue the larger circle onto the mask where the mouth should be and then glue the smaller circle on top of that.

5. Cut cardboard triangles and glue them to the mask to make Sun rays. Allow all the glue to dry.

6. Cover your work surface with newspaper. Paint the mask with brightly coloured paints. When the paint is dry, tape a large lollipop stick to the bottom of the mask on the back. To wear the mask, hold it by the stick over your face.

Burkina Faso

Burkina Faso in Africa is one of the poorest countries in the world. Farming is important to the people of Burkina Faso because most people work on farms for a living. If the crops do not grow, there will be no work or money.

Kenyan giraffe

You will need
· A3 sheet of yellow card · pencil
· pair of scissors · orange and brown
paper · glue · stapler · elastic cord

Lots of giraffes and other animals roam the plains of Kenya in Africa. This mask is simple to make and lots of fun. When you have mastered this animal mask, why not use the template on page 23 to make a lion mask?

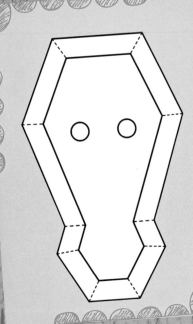

1. Copy the shape shown onto card, making sure the inner part is wide enough to cover your face. Cut out the shape. Cut out holes for the eyes, as shown on page 14.

2. Cut out shapes from the orange and brown paper. Glue them onto the mask within the inner line, so that it looks like a giraffe's face.

3. Using the template as a guide, make small cuts on the dotted lines, going up to the inner line. With the mask face down, fold up the edges. Overlap the cut edges and staple them together, but leave where the giraffe's nose meets the face unstapled.

4. Cut two horn shapes from the yellow card. Add a small piece of brown paper to the top of each horn and cut a fringe into it. Fold the bottom edge of each horn in by 2–3cm and staple the horn to the top of the mask.

Roaring fun!

Use the templates below to make a lion mask.

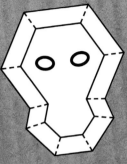

5. Cut two ears from the card. Gently bend over the top of the ear and then the end of the ear by 2–3cm. Staple the ears to the sides of the mask.

6. Measure the elastic cord so that it can go around your head. Staple it to the sides of the mask. Your mask is now ready to wear.

Egyptian mask

You will need
- paper plate, 25cm in diameter
- pair of scissors · pencil
- 2 strips of light-coloured fabric,
6cm x 22cm · double-sided tape
· newspaper · paints - including gold,
blue and brown · paintbrush
· card · stapler · large lollipop stick
· sticking tape

In Ancient Egypt, mummies wore masks made out of wood, stone or precious metals such as gold. One of the most famous masks was worn by the Pharaoh Tutankhamun. Be a Pharaoh with your own Tutankhamun mask.

1. Cut off the rim of half the paper plate. Cut out holes for the eyes, as shown on page 14.

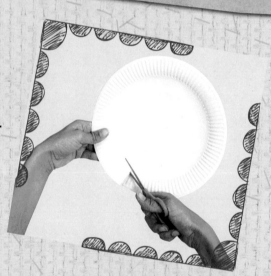

2. Use double-sided tape to stick the strips of fabric to the top of the plate, one to either side of where the rim has been trimmed off.

3. Cover your work surface with newspaper. Turn over the mask and draw a face onto the plate. Paint the plate and cloth and allow to dry.

24

4. To make a snake and vulture to decorate the mask, copy the shapes below onto card. Cut them out and paint on the details as shown. Paint the back of the vulture plain gold.

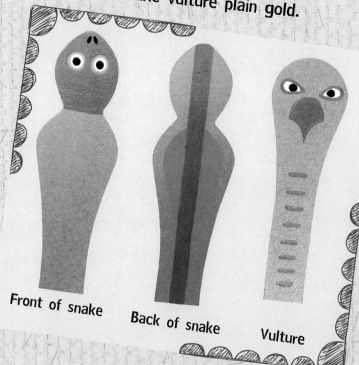

Front of snake

Back of snake

Vulture

5. When the paint is dry, gently bend the snake and vulture as shown, and staple them to the mask above the eyes.

6. Decorate the lollipop stick in gold and blue and when it is dry, tape it to the back of the mask at the bottom.

Tutankhamun

Tutankhamun became a Pharaoh when he was about nine years old. He died before he was 20. As was the tradition, he was buried with a golden mask and many treasures. His tomb was discovered in 1922 in Egypt's Valley of the Kings, more than 3,000 years after his death. Many of the Tutankhamun's treasures can be found in museums around the world.

Greek Medusa

In Ancient Greek theatres, masks helped the actors to show sadness and happiness. They also helped the men to portray women and to be more than one person in the play. Why not wear your Medusa mask and perform in your own play?

You will need
- card from cereal box · pencil
- pair of scissors · stapler · newspaper
- PVA glue · green tissue paper · paints
- paintbrushes · large lollipop stick
- strong tape

1. Cut the shape shown from the card. Cut holes for the eyes (see page 14) and mouth.

2. Cut snake shapes from the card. Staple them around the top of the head to look like hair.

3. Cover your workplace with newspaper. Twist strips of newspaper and stick them around the eyes and mouth. In the same way, add eyebrows and a nose to the mask. Scrunch up pieces of newspaper and glue them onto the snake shapes.

4. Use glue to stick on strips of tissue paper so that the whole mask is covered.

There are many stories and myths about gods and heroes that come from the Ancient Greeks. Medusa was one of the mythological characters who had hair made of snakes. Medusa's stare would turn those people who looked at her to stone.

5. When the glue is dry, paint the eyes, eyebrows and mouth. Add eyes and mouths to the snakes, too. Leave to dry.

6. Paint the lollipop stick green. When it is dry, use strong tape to stick it to the back of the mask. Your mask is now ready to wear!

Viking mask

You will need
· large balloon · shoe box · newspaper
· PVA glue · pair of scissors
· thin corrugated card · masking tape
· kitchen foil · paints and paintbrush
· stapler · strong elastic

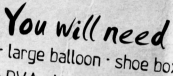

The Vikings were tough fighters, armed with spears, swords, axes, bows and arrows. They protected themselves with round wooden shields and helmets made of metal or leather. Make this Viking mask and be a ferocious Viking warrior.

1. Blow up a balloon until it is the same size as your head. Knot the balloon. Rest the balloon on the bottom half of a shoe box.

2. Cover your work surface with newspaper. Mix a small amount of water into some glue. Use this glue mixture to stick pieces of newspaper to just over one side of the balloon. Continue until you have built up about four layers. Leave overnight to dry.

3. When the glue has dried, pop the balloon and remove it from the mask. Trim the edges of the mask. Work out where the eyes and mouth need to be and cut them out.

Vikings in England

The Vikings were mainly farmers from Denmark, Norway and Sweden. They travelled great distances in longboats to conquer and settle in other countries. In 793, the Vikings arrived in north-east England on the island of Lindisfarne, where they took over a monastery.

4. Cut strips of corrugated card and glue them onto the mask to make a cross-shaped helmet.

5. Roll up pieces of newspaper to make eyebrows, a moustache and beard. Add some masking tape to hold the rolls together. Glue the rolls onto the mask and allow to dry.

6. Glue on lightly wrinkled pieces of kitchen foil to the top half of the mask, covering the card strips, too. Paint the face part of the mask and allow to dry.

7. Staple strong elastic to the sides of the mask, long enough to go around your head and to keep the mask in place.

Puppets

Contents

All about puppets

Puppets have been used for thousands of years to entertain and also to educate children. Many styles of puppet have developed from different cultures around the world.

Some of the first puppets, which were used in religious festivals, were like masks with opening and closing mouths. Another early form of puppet, believed to have started in China, is the shadow puppet. This is a flat-shaped puppet moved by rods and lit from behind. A shadow is cast onto a screen in front of an audience.

Types of puppets

Today, there are many types of puppet and they can range in size from small puppets that fit on your fingers or hands, to rod puppets (see far right) that the puppeteer moves with sticks. Japanese Bunraku puppets are so big that they need three people to work them.

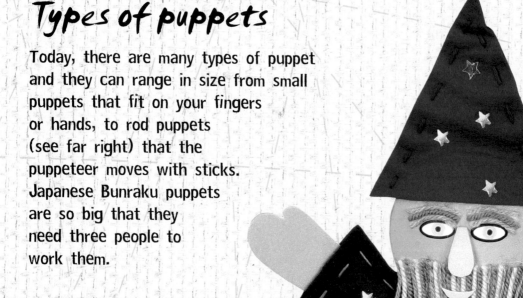

Famous puppets

Throughout history, some puppets have become famous. Often, puppets created for children become popular with adults, too. Punch and his wife Judy have been delighting audiences since the 1600s. The story of Pinocchio, written by the Italian author Carlo Collodi, has been a children's favourite since the late 1800s. Pinocchio is a marionette (a puppet that is controlled with strings by the puppeteer) that comes to life. Other popular puppets include the Muppets, with the well-loved characters Kermit the Frog and Miss Piggy.

Get started

Puppets can be made from all types of things, such as paper plates, paper bags, empty kitchen roll tubes and old socks. In this book you can discover how to make many different types of puppets. Try to use materials that you already have either at home or at school. Reusing and recycling materials like this is good for the environment and it will also save you money. The projects in this book have all been made and decorated but do not worry if yours look a little different – just have fun making and playing with your puppets.

Venus flytrap

The Venus flytrap is a flesh-eating plant. Its leaves trap insects by snapping shut as the insects land on them. The plant's digestive juices turn the insect into mush that the plant can eat. Follow these steps to make your own flesh-eating flytrap puppet.

1. Cover your work surface with a few layers of newspaper. Paint the inside of the plate red and allow it to dry. Fold the plate in half.

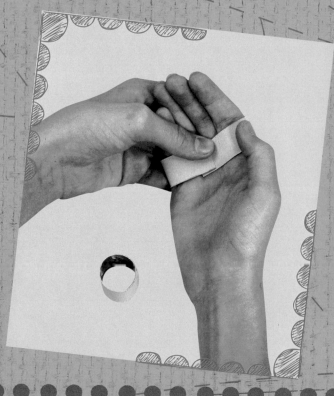

2. Curl the small strip of card around your thumb, to make a hoop through which your thumb fits. Tape the ends together. Do the same with the longer strip, this time curling it around your hand. Make sure it fits around four fingers. The hoops will be used to open and close the puppet.

3. Use double-sided tape to fix one hoop to each half of the plate. Paint the hoops and the outside of the plate green and allow them to dry.

4. Staple the straws around the edge of one half of the plate and bend them upwards.

5. Fix more straw 'teeth' to the other half of the plate so that when the trap is closed they fall between the ones on the other half of the plate.

6. Place your thumb and fingers in the hoops to open and close the flytrap. What other sort of character do you think this puppet could be?

Meat eaters

Flesh-eating or carnivorous plants like the Venus flytrap and pitcher plant grow in swamps where there is not enough goodness in the soil. They catch and eat small insects to make sure they get all the nutrients they need to live.

Safari fingers

You will need
- compass · pencil · various coloured sheets of thin card or paper · pair of scissors
- sticking tape · glue
- felt-tip pens

Finger puppets are easy to use. They sit on the ends of your fingers. Bring them to life by placing them on your middle finger and wriggling your fingertips.

FOR A LION

1. Using a compass, draw a circle onto your card which is 14cm in diameter. Cut it out and fold it into four. Cut out the quarters.

2. Curl a quarter around your finger to make a cone shape. Tape it together so that one straight edge overlaps the other straight edge.

3. Draw around the open end of the cone onto a piece of coloured paper. Use this circle as a guide and draw on a mane, as shown. Cut it out.

4. Hold the mane over the open end of the cone and stick it down onto the inside using small strips of tape.

5. To finish the lion, draw on eyes and ears or cut them out from coloured paper. Colour in the nose with a felt-tip pen.

38

FOR A RHINOCEROS

Repeat the first two steps from the lion instructions, but use different-coloured paper.

3. Cut ear shapes from coloured paper and stick them to the cone.

4. Cut out horn shapes and snip them at the bottom to make tabs, as shown. Bend the tabs in opposite directions and glue them to the cone.

5. To finish your rhino, draw on eyes or cut them out from coloured paper and stick them on.

FOR A GAZELLE

Repeat the first two steps from the lion instructions, but use different-coloured paper.

3. Cut ear shapes from coloured paper and stick them to the cone.

4. For the horns, cut out strips of paper. Wrap them around a pencil to make them curl. Stick the ends of the horns to the inside of the cone.

5. Draw on eyes or cut them out from coloured paper and glue them on. Colour in the nose with a felt-tip pen.

Endangered rhinos

Like many wild animals, the rhinoceros is endangered. In fact, the black rhino is disappearing faster than any other large animal on Earth. Unless rhinos are protected from the people who hunt them, they will become extinct.

Creepy crawly caterpillar

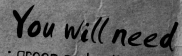

You will need
- green and yellow coloured paper
- pair of scissors · glue
- small wooden sticks · large pom-pom
- 2 stick-on eyes · small pom-pom
- 2 lollipop sticks

The caterpillar is a slow-crawling insect. Its body is made up of segments that squash up and stretch out as it moves along. Follow the steps to make this simple caterpillar rod puppet.

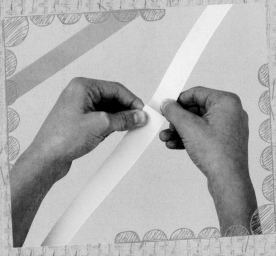

1. Cut a strip of green paper 2.5cm wide x 56cm long. You may need to stick a few strips together depending on the size paper you use. Do the same with the yellow paper.

2. Place the strips at right angles to each other so that they look like an 'L'. Stick the ends together. Fold the strips of paper over each other until you reach the end. Cut off any extra paper and stick the ends together.

3. To make antennae, glue small wooden sticks to one end of the paper spring. When the glue has dried, add a large pom-pom to make the caterpillar's head. Glue on eyes and a small pom-pom for the nose.

Life cycles

The caterpillar is one stage in the life cycle of a butterfly. The cycle begins with the butterfly laying eggs which hatch into caterpillars. When a caterpillar is ready to change, it forms a chrysalis, from which the butterfly emerges.

4. Glue a lollipop stick between the folds in the paper near the head. Glue the other stick near the tail end.

5. To make the caterpillar move, hold the sticks and move the back one towards the front one, then move the front one forward.

Scary shark

You will need

- clean old sock · felt-tip pens
- 2 stick-on eyes · double-sided tape
- sheet of white card 10cm x 16cm · pencil
- pair of scissors
- piece of grey card 7cm x 6cm

Decorating a sock is an easy way to make a puppet. Your hand and arm give the puppet movement. Here is a great way of using an old or odd sock to make a fierce puppet.

1. Put the sock over the hand you do not use to write. Put your thumb into the heel of the sock to make the bottom of the shark's mouth. Use a felt-tip pen to mark where you want to put the eyes, gills and fin.

2. Take off the sock and draw on the nose and gills. Stick on the eyes with small pieces of double-sided tape, one either side of what will be the head.

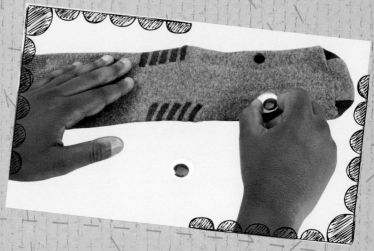

Shark facts

Sharks are fish. Like all fish, they take in oxygen from the water using gills instead of lungs. Sharks have an amazing sense of smell — more than half of a shark's brain helps it to smell!

3. Onto the white card, draw a mouth and teeth using the picture below as a guide. Cut it out.

4. Using double-sided tape, stick the mouth onto the bottom of the sock with the teeth at the toe end. Bend the teeth upwards.

5. Onto the grey card, draw a fin shape as shown. Fold the card along the dotted line. Cut out the fin and snip the bottom of the fin up the middle, up to the fold line. Fold the two halves in opposite directions to make tabs. Stick the fin to the top of the sock with double-sided tape.

6. The puppet is ready to try on! As you put the sock on, carefully fold the mouth where it naturally wants to bend. Can you make it look as though the shark is swimming in the sea?

43

Pirate shadows

A shadow puppet is usually a flat shape and is moved with rods or sticks. A light is shone behind the puppet to cast a shadow onto a screen. The audience sits in front of the screen to watch the shadows. Make your own pirate puppet and put on a show.

You will need
· A4 sheet of card · pencil · pair of scissors · pen · 6 paper fasteners (split pins) · 3 long lollipop sticks · sheet · two chairs · lamp

(1) Copy the shapes shown onto card and cut them out. Label the pieces and use a pen to mark the circles shown on the card. This is where the holes need to go. Ask an adult to help you to push the pencil through the marks to make small holes.

(2) To make the arms, push a fastener through the arm piece holes labelled F and E. Then add the hands, joining hand F to the F hole and hand E to the E hole. Open out the paper fastener.

Shadows

A shadow is made when light is blocked. Light travels in straight lines, so it cannot go around an object and it cannot travel through objects unless they are in some way see-through. As the light cannot light up the area behind the object, it forms the shadow.

3. Use paper fasteners to fix the arms to the shoulder part of the body, joining hole A to hole A and hole B to hole B.

4. In the same way fix both legs (C and D) to the bottom of the body.

5. Tape the lollipop sticks to the back of the puppet on the hands and one up the middle.

6. Using the middle stick, hold the pirate in the air. Wiggle the sticks attached to the hands to see how the puppet can move. Try hanging a sheet up between two chairs with a lamp behind you. Use the sheet as a screen for your puppet show.

Wizard glove

Glove puppets sit over the hand. Some are simple and have no arms or legs, like the sock puppet. Others have arms that are moved by the thumb and little finger. Make your own wizard glove puppet to create some magic.

You will need
· paper · pencil · pair of scissors
· different-coloured felt · artfoam
· PVA glue · needle · thread
· card or paper for eyes · felt-tip pens
· wool for beard and eyebrows
· foil stars

(1) Draw an outline of your hand onto the paper. Make sure your thumb and little finger stick out.

(2) Draw a simple person shape around the outline, making it about 2cm larger all the way around. Round off the top to give a good head shape. Cut out the shape so that you have a template.

(3) Draw around the template onto your felt and cut two pieces the same shape to give you a front and a back piece.

Get sewing

To sew a running stitch, thread a needle and tie a knot at one end of the thread. Push the point of the needle down through the fabric. Bring the needle back up again at a point further forward from where you went down. Repeat to give a row of stitches which look the same on both sides of the fabric.

4. Cut out hands for your puppet from artfoam and glue them to the back of one of the body shapes. This is the back of your wizard.

5. Place the other piece of felt over the back piece. Sew around the edge of the puppet with a running stitch (see page 46). Leave the bottom edge open.

6. Cut out a circle of artfoam for the head and glue it onto the front of the puppet. Draw eyes onto some card, cut them out and glue them on. Add a beard and eyebrows by gluing on short lengths of wool. Cut a nose and a mouth from artfoam and stick them on, too.

7. Make a hat by sewing two triangles of felt up the sides. Glue the hat to the top of the head. Use stars to decorate the wizard's outfit. When all the glue has dried, your puppet is ready to bring to life.

Chinese dragon

Dragon puppets are used in dances as part of Chinese New Year festivals. The dragons have a large head and a long tail. They are held up on sticks and carried by lots of people. Follow the steps to make your own dragon.

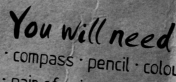

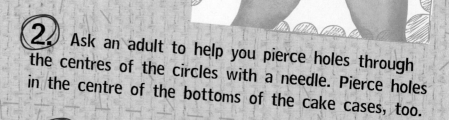

1. Use the compass to draw 26 circles that measure 6cm across on the coloured card. Cut out the circles.

2. Ask an adult to help you pierce holes through the centres of the circles with a needle. Pierce holes in the centre of the bottoms of the cake cases, too.

Chinese New Year

In China, New Year celebrations last for fifteen days at the end of January or beginning of February. People's homes are colourfully decorated and a feast of traditional foods is prepared. The fifteenth day of the New Year is marked with the Lantern Festival.

3. Knot one end of the thread. Thread the unknotted end through the hole in the centre of one circle and pull the thread through to the knot. Stick some tape over the knot to stop it slipping through the hole.

4. Thread on a cake case and another circle. Repeat this until you have used all the circles. Finish with a circle. Knot the thread and cut off any that is spare. Add a piece of tape over the knot.

5. Draw a dragon's head onto the card and colour it in. Cut it out. Cut a slit on the neck to make tabs to stick the head to one end of your dragon.

6. Draw a tail-tip onto card and cut it out. Cut a slit at the bottom to make tabs. Fold the tabs in opposite directions. Stick the tail tip to the other end of the dragon.

7. Tape a chopstick to the back of the head and another to the back of the tail.

8. The puppet is now ready to use. Move the rods and see if you can make the dragon rise and fall. It will make a great rustling sound, too!

49

Robot marionette

Marionette puppets are moved by string or wires that are attached to the arms, legs and head of the puppet. The puppeteer controls the puppet by moving a wooden bar fixed to the other end of the strings or wires.

You will need
- cardboard tube from kitchen roll
- pencil · ruler · pair of scissors
- stapler · newspaper · silver paint
- paintbrush
- 3 lengths of thin card 2cm x 10cm
- 2 lengths of thin card 2cm x 5cm
- 2 long lollipop sticks
- 2 small elastic bands · needle
- 25cm length of thick thread
- 2 33cm lengths of thick thread
- 2 45cm lengths of thick thread
- bits of coloured card · 2 stick-on eyes

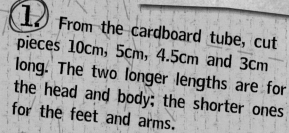

1. From the cardboard tube, cut pieces 10cm, 5cm, 4.5cm and 3cm long. The two longer lengths are for the head and body; the shorter ones for the feet and arms.

2. Take the two shorter rolls and cut each one in half to give you four arcs.

3. Roll each arc into a smaller tube and staple the ends together. The smaller ones will become the feet and the longer ones the arms. Cover your work surface with newspaper and paint all the tubes silver.

4. Using two of the longer strips of coloured card, staple one end of each to the feet of the robot and the other to the bottom of the body. Do the same with the two shorter pieces, attaching the arms to the sides at the top of the body.

5. To attach the head, staple the last strip of card from front to back at the top of the body to make a curve. Staple the head tube to the top of the curved card.

6. Make a cross with the lollipop sticks, holding them together with the elastic bands.

7. Pierce a hole in the middle of the top of the head with a needle. Pass the 25cm length thread through the hole. Knot it and stick it to the inside of the tube. Tie the other end around the middle of the crossbar.

8. Pierce a hole in the middle of the arms and legs. Knot the ends of each of the four remaining threads. Pass the two longer threads through the holes in the legs and the shorter ones through the holes in the arms. Tie the other ends to the crossbar, with the threads to the legs at the front. Tie them so that when the puppet is hanging, the threads are not too loose.

9. Add pieces of coloured card and stick-on eyes to decorate the head and body. Hold up the crossbar. Move it backwards and forwards and from side to side, to see if you can make your robot walk and flap its arms up and down.

Toys

Contents

All about toys

Today, there are many different kinds of toy to choose from. Playing with some toys means that you run and jump around, while others are more suitable for quieter play. All toys, though, are made for having fun.

Ancient toys

For thousands of years, children all over the world have been playing with toys. Before adults made toys for them, children played with everyday objects. There is evidence of stones, nuts and bones having been used as playthings in Greek and Roman times. Children in Ancient Greece and Rome also played with dolls, balls, hobbyhorses and spinning tops. These toys would have been made of wood or clay.

Toy-making and toy shops

In the 1400s in Germany, carved wooden toys began to be made in large numbers. Later, other materials, such as tin and wax, were used. Toys became a lot more affordable once new ways were found to make them in factories. By the mid 1800s, a large range of toys was available in toy shops. Toys such as dolls' houses, train sets and rocking horses were often beautifully made and very expensive to buy. Children who could not afford these ready-made toys would have played with the glass stoppers that sealed the tops of fizzy drinks bottles and rolled the iron hoops from barrels along the street.

Today's toys

Today the range of toys available to buy has grown enormously. While crazes for new toys come and go, traditional toys such as dolls and footballs are still popular. Toys today look very different from when they were first made. Many of them, including dolls like the one in the picture below, are made of plastic.

Get started!

In this book you can discover ways of making interesting toys from around the world. Try to use materials that you already have either at home or at school. For example, for the cardboard in these projects, the backs of used-up notepads, art pads and hardbacked envelopes are ideal. Reusing and recycling materials like this is good for the environment and it will save you money. The projects have all been made and decorated for this book but do not worry if yours look a little different – just have fun making and playing with your toys.

Fun yo-yo

The yo-yo was first designed in the 1920s and has remained a popular toy ever since. Yo-yo competitions are held all over the world. Adults and children perform tricks with their yo-yos to win cups and prizes.

1. Put the lid on the cardboard and draw around it. Move the lid along and draw around it again. Repeat this until you have 12 circles.

2. Cut out all the circles.

3. Glue one circle to another, until you have glued six of them together in a pile. Then do the same with the other six. Leave them to dry.

4. Stick a coloured circle onto one side of each pile of discs. Stick on coloured shapes to decorate.

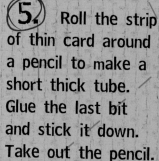

5. Roll the strip of thin card around a pencil to make a short thick tube. Glue the last bit and stick it down. Take out the pencil.

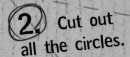

58

6. Put some glue on both ends of the cardboard tube.

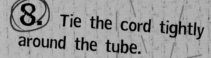

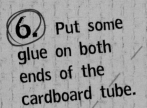

7. Stick one end of the tube onto the centre of one of the piles of card circles.

8. Tie the cord tightly around the tube.

9. Stick the undecorated side of the second pile of cards on top of the tube. Wind the rest of the cord loosely around the middle of the yo-yo and tie a loop in the end for your finger.

10. Put your finger through the loop, hold the yo-yo up in the air and let it go. Just before it reaches the floor, jerk the string and the yo-yo should roll back up the string towards your hand.

Gravity

When you let go of a yo-yo, a force called gravity pulls it towards the floor. When you jerk the string, the energy that the yo-yo has built up on the way down allows it to climb back up the string.

Racing bug

This simple wind-up toy uses an elastic band to make it move. As the elastic band unwinds, the bug crawls along the floor.

You will need
- empty cotton reel · coloured felt
- pencil · pair of scissors · PVA glue
- paintbrush · elastic band · matchstick
- sticking tape · stick-on eyes
- scraps of fake fur · black felt-tipped pen

1. Draw around the end of the cotton reel onto the felt. Cut out the circle. Do the same again so that you have two circles of felt.

2. Cut a piece of felt the same width as the cotton reel and long enough to wrap around it.

3. Cover one side of the strip of felt with glue and stick it around the cotton reel.

4. Fold one circle in half and cut a small half circle from the middle. Put glue on one side of the circle with a hole in it. Stick it onto one end of the cotton reel.

5. Thread the elastic band through the hole in the middle of the cotton reel so that a loop sticks out at each end.

6. Cut a matchstick in half. Push one half through the loop in the elastic band at the end without the felt covering. Make sure that it does not stick out over the edge of the reel. Pull the elastic band from the other end so that it is pulled tight over the matchstick. Tape it in place.

7. Using PVA glue, stick the circle of felt without the hole over the end of the cotton reel with the match in place.

8. Decorate your bug by sticking on or drawing eyes, a mouth and maybe fur or antennae.

9. Push the pencil through the loop in the elastic band. Wind up the elastic band by turning the pencil. Put the bug on a smooth surface and watch it move as the elastic band unwinds. If you make two bugs you can race them against each other.

Beastly bugs

Of all the types of animal on Earth, 95 per cent are insects! Over one million different species of insect have already been discovered. Scientists think that there might be ten times that many that have not been found yet.

Jumping Jack

Jumping figures are believed to be among the earliest forms of mechanical toys. Similar toys were first made of wood thousands of years ago in Ancient Egypt.

You will need

- piece of stiff card 21cm x 29.5cm
- pencil · pair of scissors · glue
- green sticky-backed paper · red sticky-backed paper · yellow sticky-backed paper · black sticky-backed paper
- paints · black felt-tip pen or black ballpoint pen · paintbrush · 2 paper fasteners · piece of red wool, about 60cm long · large sewing needle · large button

1. To make the shapes of a head and body, draw one small and one large circle, joined together, on the stiff card. Draw a triangular shape on the stiff card to fit the head — this will be the hat. Cut out these pieces and stick the hat onto the head.

2. Draw two curving 'L' shapes on the stiff card, which will be the arms and legs. Add on two little round shapes for the hand and shape the shoes.

3. Draw around the legs onto green sticky-backed paper and cut them out. Draw around the bottom of the body circle onto the same green paper and cut it out. Stick the cut-out pieces onto the legs and body. Cut out two strips of the same green paper to make braces.

4. Place the card onto the red sticky-backed paper, draw around the hat and cut out the shape. Cut straight across the bottom. Stick the shape onto the hat.

5. Draw around the arms onto yellow sticky-backed paper and cut these out. On the same paper, draw around the top of the body (cut straight across the neckline). Stick these shapes onto the arms and top of the body.

Jumping Jacks use simple levers to make them move. As you pull down on the wool, it forces the other end of the cardboard shape up in the air. The middle of a lever is called the pivot point. The paper fastener is at the pivot point in this Jumping Jack.

6. Cut out black sticky-backed paper feet and stick those on. Stick the braces onto the yellow top. Paint the face.

7. Using a pencil, make a small hole in each arm and leg piece, just on the outer bend. Make a slightly bigger hole on the inner bend of each arm and leg piece and two holes on the body. Thread the needle and then pass it through the small holes on the arm and leg pieces. Leave the ends hanging for now.

8. Push paper fasteners through the bigger holes on the braces, arms and legs. Open them out at the back of your figure.

9. Thread the loose ends of the wool through a button and tie a knot. Now pull on the button to make Jack jump up and down!

Beanbag frog

You will need
- paper · pencil · pair of scissors · pins
- 2 pieces of felt · sewing thread
- needle · rice · buttons, beads or stick-on eyes · glue · felt scraps

Children have played with stuffed toys for thousands of years. Toys can be stuffed with many different kinds of materials. This beanbag frog is stuffed with rice to make it floppy.

1. Fold the piece of paper in half and copy the shape of half a frog onto it. Cut out the shape and use it as a pattern.

2. Open out the pattern and lay it on one of the pieces of felt. Pin it in place so that it cannot move. Cut out the shape. Remove the pins and pattern.

3. Repeat step 2 with the second piece of felt.

4. Put the two frog-shaped pieces of felt on top of each other. Using backstitch (see panel), stitch all the way around the frog 1cm from the edge, following the outline. Stop sewing 3cm away from where you started.

5. Turn the frog inside out. To stuff the frog, fill it with rice. Do not over-stuff the frog or it will be too stiff.

Backstitch

To sew backstitch, tie a knot in the end of the thread. Push the needle up from the back of the fabric and pull the thread through to the knot. Push the point of the needle back down through the fabric, just behind where the thread has come up. Pull it to make a stitch. Push the needle up from the back to just in front of the first stitch and pull it through. Push the needle back down to join up with the last stitch. A row of backstitches will all join up together.

6. Sew up the gap by making stitches from the back to the front over and over again.

7. Decorate your frog by sticking on eyes or buttons and gluing on felt spots.

Racing car

Ever since the car was invented, model cars have been favourite toys. The steps below will show you how to make a magnetic car and a track to drive it around.

You will need
- sheet of card 45cm x 30cm
- paints · paintbrushes
- 4 bottle tops all the same size
- PVA glue · 2 matchboxes
- pair of scissors · masking tape
- sharp pencil · piece of dowel
- 4 black bottle tops · long ruler
- non-drying modelling clay
- pair of magnets that stick together

1. Paint a racetrack on the card. Leave it to dry.

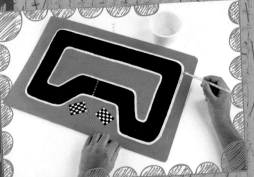

2. Glue the four bottle tops onto the underside of the race track, one in each corner.

3. To make a car, take the tray out of one of the matchboxes. Cut a triangle shape from each side of the box.

4. To make the front of the car, tape the top of the box to the base.

5. Flatten the outer sleeve of the second box and tape it to the back of the first box to make a 'spoiler'.

6. Using a sharp pencil, make holes in both sides of the car at the front and the back.

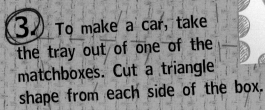

7. Paint and decorate the car.

8. Cut two pieces of dowel long enough to go right through the width of the car plus 3cm.

9. To make the wheels, fill the black bottle tops with clay. Push the end of a piece of dowel into the centre of the clay. Then push it through the holes in the front of the box and into another bottle top, filled with clay. Do the same with the back wheels.

10. Tape one magnet to the underside of the car and the other magnet to the end of the ruler.

11. Slide the ruler under the sheet of card and move your car around the track. You could make two cars and race with a friend.

Magic magnets

Magnets are surrounded by a force called a magnetic field. This invisible force can 'attract' the magnets (pull them toward each other) or 'repel' them (push them away from each other). As you move the ruler the two magnets attract and pull the car round the track.

Penguin family

Stacking or nesting toys are traditionally dolls. Make a set of stacking shapes and decorate them to look like an animal or bird.

1. Cut three or four pieces of modelling clay — each one increasing in size. Roll each of the pieces into a cylinder shape. The shapes must be fatter as well as taller as they get bigger.

2. Roll the end of each cylinder under your hand to make the shape a bit narrower at the top. Stand the shapes upright.

3. Wrap each shape tightly in cling film.

Russian dolls

In Russia, traditional stacking dolls are called Matryoshka. There are at least five dolls in a set and sometimes many more. The dolls are made of hollow wood. Each doll opens in the middle and stacks inside another. Traditional dolls are painted like women and children in Russian costume.

4. Tear or cut some newspaper into small pieces.

5. Mix a blob of glue with the same amount of water.

6. Stick the pieces of newspaper all over the clay figures except for the base. This is called papier mâché. Make sure that the figures are completely covered with at least three layers of papier mâché. Leave them to dry overnight. Pull on the cling film to remove the clay from the papier mâché.

7. Peel off the cling film. Paint your papier mâché figures. These figures are painted to look like a family of penguins but you could choose to decorate them to look like any group of animals or birds.

Kaleidoscope

You will need
- cardboard sweet tube, 5cm wide
- pencil · coloured paper · pair of scissors
- PVA glue · 3 pieces of plastic mirror the length of the tube x 4cm wide
- masking tape · piece of clear acetate
- thin card · small beads and sequins

A kaleidoscope uses coloured glass and mirrors to make beautiful repeating patterns. The patterns change as you turn the kaleidoscope around.

1. Push one end out of the tube. With a sharp pencil, make a hole in the other end.

2. Cut a piece of coloured paper the same length as the tube and wide enough to wrap around it. Decorate the paper with cut-out coloured shapes.

3. Put the strips of mirror face down, side by side. Using masking tape, stick the strips of mirror together.

4. Fold the pieces of mirror into a triangle. Keep the mirrored surface on the inside. Using masking tape, stick the triangle together.

5. Push the mirror triangle inside the tube.

6. Cut a strip of card 2cm wide that fits round the tube and overlaps by 1cm. Glue or tape the card into a hoop.

7. Cut out one circle of acetate slightly larger than the end of the tube. Stick the card hoop onto the the acetate circle.

8. Put the beads and sequins into the card hoop. Cut a circle of thin card slightly larger than the end of the tube. Stick it on top of the hoop to make a box.

9. Stick the acetate base of the box with the beads inside onto the open end of the tube.

10. Look through the hole at the end of the tube and roll the tube around. You will see the shapes change as different beads are reflected in the mirrors.

Tube of mirrors

As you look through a kaleidoscope the jumble of beads at the end are transformed into regular patterns. The mirrors inside the kaleidoscope reflect a small section of the beads, making it look as though there are six symmetrical pictures.

Carousel

The first carousel, or merry-go-round, was built in Europe in 1800 and was known as a ring of flying horses. It became a popular attraction at fairs, seaside resorts and amusement parks.

You will need

· a small motor · non-drying modelling clay · 2 crocodile clips · 3 circles of artfoam, 11cm across · 2 circles of thin card, 11cm across · rolling pin · coloured paper · pair of scissors · glue · battery in a battery holder · hole punch · 5 pieces of dowel, 8cm long · circle of card, 12cm across

1. Push the motor into a ball of clay and push the clay onto a hard surface to fix it in place.

2. Connect one end of each of the crocodile clips to the connectors on the motor.

3. Make a pile with the three circles of artfoam at the top and a circle of thin card at the bottom.

4. Roll out a ball of clay 5mm thick and put it on top of the artfoam.

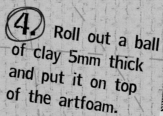

5. Cut a strip of coloured paper long enough to wrap around the circles. Glue it on.

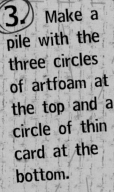

6. Push the spindle of the motor through the centre of the thin card circle and into the artfoam.

7. Turn the motor over and fix the clay to a hard surface. Connect up the loose crocodile clips to the ends of the battery. The base of the carousel will start to spin. If it is spinning too fast, add another layer of clay until it is spinning slowly. When you have the correct speed, take off one of the battery connectors.

8. Punch five holes in the remaining small circle of card. Put it on top of the clay. Push the dowels through the holes into the clay base.

9. Cut a piece of coloured paper to fit around the outside of the larger circle of card. Stick this circle on top of the dowels. Cut out horse or car shapes and stick them onto the dowels.

10. Carefully put the carousel onto the spindle on top of the motor. Connect up the loose crocodile clip to the battery and your carousel should turn. Do not run the carousel continuously.

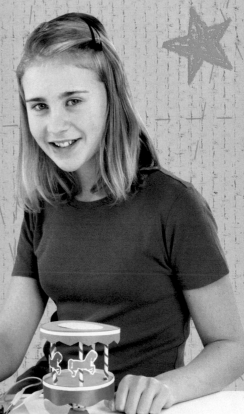

Badge holder

Fabric is great for making books because it is strong and can be washed. In this project you can make your own fabric book for keeping your favourite badges safe.

1. Cut one large, one medium and one small rectangle from the felt. If you have a pair of pinking shears then use these instead of scissors as they give a zig-zag effect.

2. Lay the rectangles on top of each other, with the largest one at the bottom and the smallest one at the top. Staple them together down the middle.

Fab felt

Felt is a fabric made from wool. This means that it is good for making hats and clothes that keep you warm. It is used in Mongolia, where it is extremely cold, to make tents known as yurts.

3. Fold the end of one length of ribbon over and staple it halfway up the side of the front cover of the book. Do the same with the other length of ribbon, this time stapling it to the back cover. Be careful not to staple the pages together.

4. To decorate the front cover, cut out and glue on shapes of felt.

5. You can now start pinning your badges on the felt pages to keep your collection safe.

Hallowe'en bag

What we know as Hallowe'en was originally part of the Celtic celebration of New Year, known as Samhain. Today on Hallowe'en, people carve pumpkins and many children dress up in costumes, going from door to door trick or treating. Follow these simple steps to make your own pumpkin-shaped treat bag to hold all your goodies.

1. From the long edge of the orange artfoam, measure and cut out a strip that is 10cm wide and 40cm long. From the remaining artfoam, cut two circles that are about 20cm in diameter. You may find it helpful to draw around a plate for this.

2. Place the edge of one circle against the edge of the strip of artfoam. Staple them together, about 1cm in from the edge. Continue stapling around the circle, keeping the edges together.

3. Staple on the second circle in the same way.

4. Draw and cut out shapes at the opened end of both circles to make handles.

5. To give your pumpkin bag a face, cut out eye, nose and mouth shapes from the black artfoam. Using double-sided tape, stick them to the bag. Your bag is ready to fill with delicious treats! You could change the colour and decorations on this bag to make a bag for Easter or Christmas.

The light season

The Celtic year was divided into two seasons: the light and the dark. The last day of October was the end of the light season and the end of the year. The Celts believed that on 31 October, the dead would visit the places where they used to live. To protect themselves and to scare away unfriendly spirits, the Celts carved images into turnips. Today on Hallowe'en, people carve pumpkins instead.

Musical Instruments

Contents

All about musical instruments

People have used musical instruments for thousands of years to make tuneful and rhythmic sounds. They are played in many different ways all over the world.

Types of instruments

There are four different groups of musical instrument: percussion, string, wind and keyboard. Percussion instruments, such as drums and cymbals, can be hit, clashed together, shaken or even scraped to produce a sound. String instruments, such as the violin and harp, give out a sound from their strings when played with a bow or plucked with the fingers. The strings are stretched over a hollow wooden box which makes the sound louder. Wind instruments, including the flute and trumpet (see below), are tubes made from wood or metal that the player blows into. This is sometimes through a reed, or by vibrating the lips, like blowing a raspberry, into a mouthpiece. Keyboard instruments, such as the piano and synthesizer, use sets of keys, levers and buttons which are pressed down to hammer out a note.

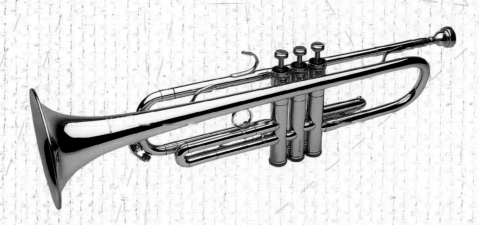

Culture and music

Music plays an important role in many cultures and religions. For example, Spanish dancers use instruments known as castanets while dancing the flamenco. In Africa, ankle rattles, sometimes made from insect cocoons with seeds or stones inside them, are worn during tribal dances. Dancers shake the rattles to add rhythm. Tribesmen of the rainforests in South America dance with an instrument called the rainmaker, made from the hollow stems of dried cactus plants. They rattle it to call on the gods to bring rain. In the Buddhist religion, bells and drums give ceremonies a rythmic beat.

Get started

In this book you can discover ways of making interesting musical instruments from around the world. Try to use materials that you already have either at home or at school. For example, for the cardboard in these projects, the backs of used-up notepads, writing pads, art pads and hardbacked envelopes are ideal. Reusing and recycling materials like this is good for the environment and it will save you money. The projects have all been made and decorated for this book but do not worry if yours look a little different — just have fun making and playing your instruments.

Spanish castanets

You will need

- piece of coloured card 15cm x 8cm
- 2 buttons about 4cm wide · pencil
- pair of scissors · coloured paper
- glue · 50cm length of cord · masking tape · sticky pads

Castanets are percussion instruments that are held in the hand. They are used in flamenco dancing to tap out a rhythm. Can you click out your own rhythm with these fun castanets?

1. Fold the card in half. Put a button in the centre of one side of the card. Draw the shape shown around it, making sure the circular part is wider than the button. With the card still folded, cut out the shape but do not cut along the fold.

2. Cut out shapes from the coloured paper and glue them on to the outside of the castanets.

3. Tie a double knot at each end of the cord. Stick the middle of the cord to the inside of the fold with masking tape.

4. Tie the cord around the fold as shown. Remember, it needs to be loose enough to fit two fingers under it.

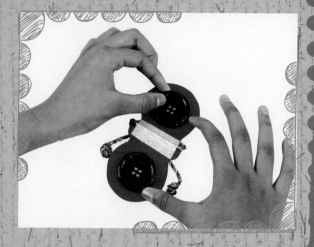

5. Use the sticky pads to attach buttons to the insides of the castanets.

6. Your castanets are now ready to play. Slip your first two fingers between the cord and the castanets. Then use your fingers to knock the two halves together against your palm. How fast can you click them?

Get dancing!

Flamenco dancers hold a set of castanets in each hand. Those in the right hand have a higher sound or pitch and are known as hembra (female). The castanets in the left hand are lower in pitch and are called macho (male).

Simple flute

You will need
· 4 strips of paper, each 3cm x 8cm
· masking tape · 2 clean long lollipop
sticks · pair of scissors · greaseproof
paper · coloured tape

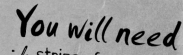

The flute is a wind instrument, so notes are made by blowing into it. This flute is easy to make and does not need many materials. When you have made it, try blowing out your favourite tunes.

1. Fold each strip of paper in half three times to make a short block.

2. Tape two blocks of paper the same distance in from either end of one of the lollipop sticks. Now do the same for the other stick.

3. Cut a rectangle of greaseproof paper that is twice the width of the sticks and long enough to cover the paper blocks. Fold it in half along the longest length.

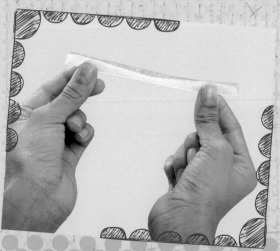

Wind power

The first wind instruments were made from animal bones with holes down the side, a bit like today's recorders. Since then, wind instruments have been made from wood and metal.

4. Place a lollipop stick in front of you with the paper blocks facing upward. Lay the strip of greaseproof paper on top of the stick and tape it to the ends of the stick. Make sure the greaseproof paper is as straight and as tight as possible.

5. Lay the second lollipop stick on top of the other stick with the paper blocks facing downwards. Wrap some tape around both lollipop sticks to hold everything together.

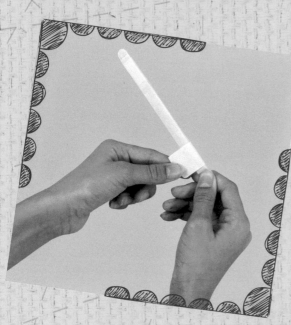

6. Blow through the sticks with the folded edge of greaseproof paper towards you. This makes the surfaces of the greaseproof paper vibrate, producing a noise. If you gently squeeze the sticks together as you blow, you can change the pitch of the note.

Bongo drums

Bongo drums are believed to have come from Cuba and are traditionally made from two different-sized drums. Make these colourful bongos and beat out your favourite song.

1. Cut down one side and across the bottom of the carrier bag so that you have a single layer of plastic. Put a tube on the plastic and draw around it. Cut out the circle, adding an extra 5cm all around. Do the same for the second tube.

2. Place a circle of plastic over the open end of a tube. Using pieces of masking tape, stick the plastic down all around the side. Keep pulling the plastic tightly as you do this. Wrap another piece of tape around the tube to make sure the plastic is stuck firmly. Do the same with the second tube.

Make some noise!

The drums are different sizes so that they make different sounds. The sound a drum makes also depends on its shape, what it is made from and how tight the skin at the top of the drum is.

3. Cut a sheet of coloured paper large enough to go around each tube. Decorate it with different shapes and colours of paper. Wrap the decorated sheets around the tubes and glue them down.

4. Stick the two strips of cardboard together, end-to-end with each strip overlapping the other by 4cm.

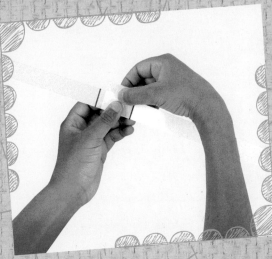

5. Fold up either side of the overlap and fix tape around the ends of the strips to form a triangle. Decorate the triangle by painting it. Stick the triangle to the tubes with double-sided tape, making sure the base of the triangle is at the top of the tubes.

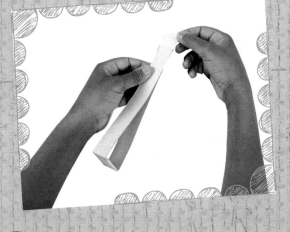

6. To play the bongos, put them between your knees and gently tap the tops with your fingertips. Can you hear a different sound from each drum?

Jazz washboard

Washboards were originally used for washing clothes. People doing their laundry noticed that the corrugated surface made a good sound when they scraped their fingers over it.

You will need
- A4-sized piece of stiff card
- pencil · ruler · pair of scissors
- corrugated paper. 15cm x 17cm
- glue · 2 strips of corrugated card. 3cm x 30cm · 2 strips of corrugated card. 3cm x of 15cm · newspaper
- paint · paintbrush

1. Draw a line across the stiff card 3cm from the top. Then draw lines down the card, 3cm in from either side. Draw a line across the card 10cm from the bottom.

2. Draw another line 7cm from the bottom of the card and cut around it, making sure you are left with the shape shown.

3. Glue down the corrugated paper in the centre of your frame, making sure that the grooves go across the frame.

Spoons, kazoos and jugs

Washboards are played by musicians in a jug band. Members of a jug band play instruments made from things found in the home, such as a jug, spoons and a kazoo. A kazoo is a comb covered in tissue paper that is blown across to make a tune. What other things from around your house could you use to make music?

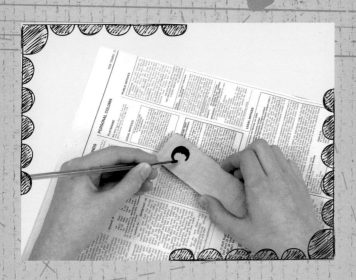

4. Cover your work surface with newspaper. Use paint to decorate the strips of corrugated card and leave them to dry.

5. When the paint has dried, glue the two long strips of corrugated card one to either side of the washboard. Then glue the two short strips across the top and bottom. When the glue has dried, the washboard is ready to play.

6. Use a pencil to scrape up and down the washboard. Experiment with short and long scrapes to see what sort of tune you can make.

African thumb piano

Thumb pianos are played by plucking keys. The keys are fixed to a wooden box or a hollowed gourd. Follow these steps to make a thumb piano and create a gentle melody.

You will need

· 2 squares of stiff card 10cm x 10cm, plus some spare · 6 clean wooden coffee stirrers · glue · ruler · newspaper · paint · paintbrush · empty shoe box with lid

1. Place one of the card squares down on your work surface. Arrange five of the stirrers so that they match those in the picture.

2. Glue the first stirrer down in place. Glue the next stirrer 1.5cm further out over the end of the card. Glue down the remaining stirrers, moving each one out another 1.5cm further than the previous one.

3. Measure out six 10cm-long strips from the spare card, wide enough to fit the gaps between the stirrers. Cut them out and glue them onto the card between the stirrers.

4. Glue the other square of card over the top to cover the stirrers and leave to dry.

5. Cover your work surface with newspaper. Paint the square. With the end of the spare wooden stirrer scratch a design into the square. Leave the square to dry. Then paint alternate keys black.

6. When all the paint has dried, place the piano on top of the shoe box which will act as a soundbox. Hold down the piano with one hand while you twang the keys with your fingers on the other. Experiment on different surfaces to see if you can create different sounds.

Good vibrations

Any sound we hear is a result of something moving. With the thumb piano, the quivering movement, known as vibration, of the plucked sticks makes the sound. Vibrations are made louder, or amplified, with the use of a hollow container, known as a soundbox.

Hand drum

You will need
- 2 shoelaces, about 35cm long
- empty cardboard cheese-triangle tub
- stapler · masking tape · pair of scissors
- paint and paintbrush · coloured card
- glue · double-sided tape · 1m length of wide ribbon

The chod drum is a small, double-sided hand drum. It is used by Buddhist monks during meditation. To play the drum, you need to twist your hand so that the knots swing from side to side, hitting the drumheads.

1. Staple one end of each lace onto the inside of the bottom of the tub. The laces need to be directly opposite each other. Stick a piece of tape over each staple.

2. Cut each lace so that it reaches beyond the middle of the base of the tub. Make a knot at the end of each shoelace.

3. Put the lid back on the tub with the laces hanging on the outside of it. Tape the tub shut all the way around, taping over the laces.

4. Paint the rims of the tub and allow them to dry. Glue a strip of coloured card around the side of the tub.

5. Cut circles of card big enough to cover the lid and bottom of the tub. Stick the card down and decorate it with shapes of coloured card.

6. Stick double-sided tape around the edge of the tub. Place the tub on your work surface with the lid facing upwards and the laces on the left and right.

7. Stick down the centre of the length of ribbon at the far side of the tub edge. Then stick the ribbon around the edge. Staple the ribbon together where the ends meet at the bottom.

8. The hand drum is now ready to play. Hold onto the ribbon, and place your fingertips at the bottom of the drum. Twist your wrist and watch the laces swing from side to side.

Chanting monks

Buddhists are people who follow the religious beliefs of a man called Siddhartha Gautama. Buddhist monks are men who give up their possessions and family to spend time studying holy books, chanting and meditating.

Shaking maracas

You will need

For each maraca: · newspaper
· small balloon · small beaker
· PVA glue mixed with water
(see box on page 97)
· small pieces of white paper
· pair of scissors · funnel
· 2 tablespoons of dry rice · thin card
· small stapler · masking tape
· paints and paintbrush.

Maracas are popular in Latin America. They were originally made from hollowed-out gourds that had been left to dry. The steps below make one maraca, so you will need to repeat the instructions to make another one.

1. Begin by laying out sheets of newspaper over your work area. Blow up a balloon to the size you would like your maraca to be and knot it. Rest it on a beaker with the knotted part facing upwards.

2. To papier mâché the balloon, stick bits of newspaper with lots of the glue and water mixture onto the balloon. Leave a space around the knot. When you have built four layers over the balloon, go over it with a layer of white paper. Leave the balloon to dry.

3. When the balloon is dry, hold onto the knot and carefully pop the balloon with a pair of scissors. Remove any pieces of balloon stuck in the paper shell. Rest the shell on the beaker with the hole at the top. Use the funnel to pour in the rice.

4. To make a handle for the maraca, roll up the thin card into a tube. It must be big enough to sit over the hole of the ball and long enough for you to hold.

5. Fix the handle together using a stapler. Then snip a short way up around one end of the tube. Fan the snipped bits out. Sit the fanned end over the hole in the ball and stick it down with pieces of tape. Tape up the other end of the handle.

6. Papier mâché the handle with a few layers of white paper.

7. While the handle is drying, make the second maraca by repeating steps one to six. When both are completely dry, paint the maracas with brightly coloured patterns. When the paint is dry, have a dance and shake your maracas.

Get crafty!

Papier mâché is a way of creating shapes from paper and a glue mixture which, when dry, are hard and can be painted. Your mixture of PVA glue and water should be more runny than glue but not watery. Try adding the water a teaspoon at a time to make sure you do not add too much water.

Egyptian harp

You will need
- small shoe box · pair of scissors
- wooden coat hanger with removable hook · pencil · 4 paper fasteners (split pins) · very strong tape
- coloured card · paint · paintbrush
- double-sided tape · 4 long elastic bands

Harps were played in Ancient Egypt. They came in many different shapes and sizes. Some had only a few strings while others had more than 20. This Egyptian harp takes time to make, but it is well worth it!

1. Take the lid off the shoe box. Cut a slit just over halfway down the middle of one end of the box, as wide as the edge of the hanger.

2. Mark four points down the middle length of the top of the lid. Push through a paper fastener at each point and open it up on the underside. Put the lid back onto the box and tape around it to seal the box. Do not tape over the slit.

3. Using the picture as a guide, draw an animal's head on the coloured card. Draw the neck slightly longer so that you can stick it to the box. Cut out the head and decorate it. Decorate the rest of the box.

Egyptians and mummies

Animals were very important to the Ancient Egyptians. They believed that some animals had supernatural powers. Often when the animals died, they were mummified, so that they could be buried with their owners.

98

4. Cut a 1cm slit at the bottom of the head to make tabs. Bend the tabs in opposite directions. Stick the head to the end of the box without the slit with double-sided tape.

5. Ask an adult to help you to remove the hook from the coat hanger. Using strong tape, stick an elastic band onto the centre of the hanger. Tape on three more elastic bands as shown.

6. Ask an adult to help you with this step. Push the end of the hanger without the elastic bands into the slit at the back of the box. Rest it on the bottom of the box. While holding the hanger up, stretch the lowest elastic band to hook it onto nearest fastener. Repeat with the other elastic bands, each time moving up the hanger and hooking onto the next fastener.

7. The harp is now ready to play. Either rest it on a table or place it between your knees and pluck the elastic bands. Can you play a gentle tune?

Cards

Contents

Season's Greetings

All about cards

The Ancient Egyptians and the Chinese sent the very first greetings cards. The Egyptians wrote their messages on a type of paper made from the leaves of a plant called papyrus. The early Chinese people exchanged messages of goodwill at Chinese New Year. In the mid 1400s, cards began to be printed on paper. The first-known greetings card in existence is a Valentine card made at around this time. It is now on display in the British Museum. These early printed cards were very expensive to buy and were delivered by hand.

New techniques

In the 1870s, a new printing technique meant that greetings cards could be printed in full colour. Since then, handwritten notes and handmade cards have largely given way to mass-produced greetings cards. Pop-up cards, pull-the-tab cards and turn-the-wheel cards added extra interest to the simple folded card. Now, the most frequently sent cards are Christmas cards and birthday cards.

Help the environment

Today, to save energy and help the environment, some people prefer to design their own e-cards on a computer and send them by e-mail. Cards are still sent through the post, and people often recycle the cards they receive. New cards can be made using the recycled paper.

Get started

In this book you can discover ways of making lots of interesting cards. Try to use materials that you already have either at home or at school. For example, for the cardboard in these projects, the backs of used up notepads, art pads and hardbacked envelopes are ideal. Reusing and recycling materials like this is good for the environment and it will save you money. The projects have all been made and decorated for this book but do not worry if yours look a little different — just have fun making and giving your cards.

Printed card

You will need
- sheet of artfoam · pair of scissors
- cardboard tube · glue or double-sided
  tape · ruler · paint · flat tray · piece
  of stiff card · newspaper · piece of
  folded card

This card is made using a simple form of block printing. In block printing, patterns are made by printing from blocks with shapes carved into them. Different colours can be printed on top of each other.

1. Cut simple shapes such as leaves, flowers, cars or animals from the artfoam.

2. Stick the shapes onto the cardboard tube. Leave about 3cm without any shapes at each end of the tube.

3. Put a blob of paint onto the tray. Using the piece of stiff card, spread out the paint into a thin layer.

4. Roll the cardboard tube along the tray so that the shapes become coated in paint.

5. Put the folded card onto some newspaper. The side onto which you want to print should be facing up. Gently roll the tube over the card so that the paint from the shapes prints on the card but the tube does not touch the paper. Leave your card to dry.

Block printing

The very first printed books were made using carved wooden blocks. Words and pictures were carved into blocks of wood. Ink was rolled onto the wooden block and the block was pressed onto paper. The blocks could be used over and over again.

Surprise card

Christmas cards have always been among the most popular cards. Follow the steps below to make a Christmas cracker card with a hidden surprise.

You will need

· strip of thin red card, 42cm x 7cm · ruler
· piece of thin yellow card, 9cm x 6cm
· pair of scissors · pencil
· 2 strips of paper, 10cm x 1cm · PVA glue
· paintbrush · coloured paper

① Fold each end of the red card in towards the centre, 10cm from the end.

② Turn the card over. Fold it back the other way, 15.5cm from each end. Open out the card.

③ Snip out triangles from the edge of the piece of yellow card to make it jagged. Write the word 'Surprise!' on it.

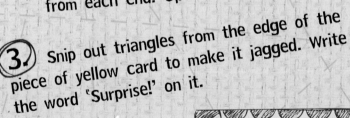

④ To make the spring, put the ends of the two strips of paper together at right angles. Glue them together.

5. Fold the bottom strip over the top strip and crease it. Keep doing this until the paper strips are all folded up.

6. Brush some PVA glue on the second-last piece of folded paper and stick the last piece down onto it. Stick the spring in the centre of the red card. Stick the yellow jagged card on top of it.

7. Turn the card over and cut out a triangle shape at the top and bottom of the card on each side, 4.5cm from each end. You now have a cracker shape with 'Surprise!' hidden inside. Decorate the cracker with coloured paper shapes. Fold up the card. As you pull the ends of the cracker the 'Surprise!' will jump out and wobble.

PRISE!

Christmas cards

The world's first printed Christmas card was designed in England in 1843 by John Callcott Horsley. More than 2,000 cards were printed and sold that year, priced at a shilling each.

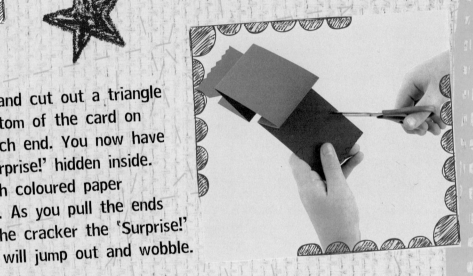

Pop-up card

For thousands of years, many cultures have used candles to celebrate all sorts of occasions, from birthdays to religious festivals and important ceremonies. You can adapt this candle card to wish people whatever you choose!

1. Fold the larger piece of card in half. Rub along the fold to crease the card.

2. Fold the second piece of card in half. Fold the bottom edge up to the top and crease it. Turn the card over and do the same on the other side.

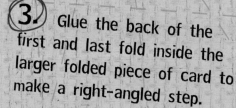

3. Glue the back of the first and last fold inside the larger folded piece of card to make a right-angled step.

4. Take the yellow card and, using a ruler and pencil, draw four fat candles on top of a cake. Draw lightly so that you can erase any pencil marks later. Carefully cut around the candles and cake. Take your time, especially around the flames and the edge of the cake.

5. Cut out four flame shapes from the orange sticky-backed paper. They must be smaller than the yellow flames. Stick the orange flames onto the yellow candle flames. Draw tiny lines with coloured glitter glue or a red felt-tip pen in the centre of the flames to look like glowing wicks. Glue the piece of metallic blue paper onto the centre of the cake shape.

6. Glue the candles to the 'step' inside your card. Then write your message, outside and inside your pop-up card.

HAPPY BIRTHDAY!

Paper engineering

Pop-up greetings cards were very popular in Europe in the late 18th century. The technique was developed to be used in pop-up books and adapted to create elaborate Christmas and Valentine's cards. A person who designs cards or books with moving parts is called a paper engineer.

Pull-tab card

Follow these steps to make your own pull-tab greetings card. By pulling the tab you can change the clown's expression from sad to happy.

You will need
· A4 piece of yellow card · ruler
· pencil · pair of scissors · eraser
· double-sided tape
· A5 piece of white card
· piece of white card 3cm x 4cm
· coloured paper · glue
· red and black felt-tip pens

1. Fold the card in half along the longest side. On the front of the card draw two lines 4cm from the long edges. Draw one horizontal line 9cm from the top of the card and another 8cm from the bottom of the card. The four points where the lines meet will make a rectangular shape.

2. Cut out the rectangle from the middle of the card. Rub out the pencil lines.

3. Use double-sided tape to stick together the side opposite the fold and the bottom edge of the card.

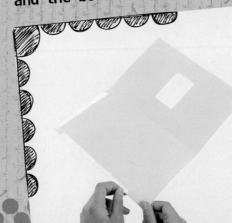

112

4. Stick the small piece of white card to the top of the larger piece to make a tab. Slide the white card inside the yellow card. Cut out coloured shapes and stick them onto the front of the card to make a clown face like the one in the picture. Draw a sad mouth in the rectangle onto the white card.

5. Using the tab pull up the white card so that you can no longer see the sad mouth shape. Draw a happy mouth shape onto the white card. Push the white card back inside the card so that the sad mouth is showing.

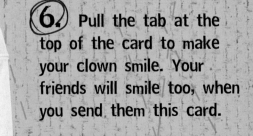

Clown make-up

White-faced clowns are what most people think of when they think of circus clowns. Every clown creates his or her own face make-up design. Once a clown starts to use a design in his or her performances, no other clown is allowed to copy it.

6. Pull the tab at the top of the card to make your clown smile. Your friends will smile too, when you send them this card.

Padded card

In the early 1800s, Valentine cards were made by hand. The cards were made using lace, silks and satins. Popular designs for these cards were hearts, roses and pictures of Cupid. Follow the steps below to sew your own Valentine card.

You will need
- piece of coloured card 30cm x 15cm
- piece of paper 11cm x11cm · pencil
- pair of scissors · 2 pieces of coloured felt each 11cm x 11cm · pins
- 2 smaller pieces of felt in different colours · needle and thread
- cotton wool · glue · ribbon

1. Fold the card in half along the longest side.

2. Fold the paper in half and draw half of a heart shape. Cut around the shape. Unfold it so that you have a whole heart shape.

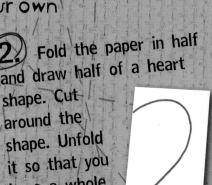

3. Put the two larger pieces of felt together and pin the paper heart onto them. Cut around the shape.

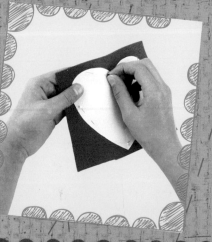

4. Unpin the paper heart from the felt and fold it in half again. Draw half of a smaller heart shape inside the first one. Cut it out and unfold it.

5. Pin the smaller paper heart onto one of the smaller pieces of felt and cut around it.

6. Follow steps 4 and 5 again, this time making an even smaller heart shape.

7. Using a running stitch (see panel), sew the two biggest heart shapes together. Before you sew all the way around the shape, push a small amount of cotton wool into the heart.

8. Finish off the stitching by doing the last stitch twice. Push the needle down through the fabric to the back.

9. Stick the big remaining heart onto the padded heart. Glue the small heart on top. Put glue on the back of the padded heart and stick it onto the card. Decorate the card with a neat ribbon bow and more felt hearts.

Running stitch

To sew running stitches, thread a needle and tie a knot in the end of the thread. Push the needle through from the back of the fabric and pull the thread until the knot stops it going any further. Then push the point of the needle back through the front of the fabric, just in front of where the thread has come through. Pull it to make a stitch. To make a row of running stitches look really good, keep the stitches and the spaces between them all the same length.

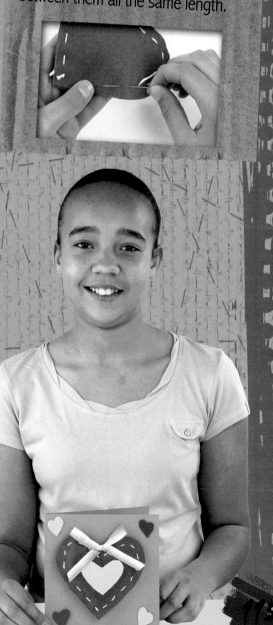

Photo card

A card with a disc that moves around can be used to display your favourite photographs. You can use this type of card for any occasion.

You will need

- piece of card 30cm x 15cm
- compass · pencil · ruler
- piece of card in a different colours, 15cm x 15cm
- pair of scissors · paper fastener
- photographs or pictures that you want to display
- glue · coloured paper

1. Fold the bigger piece of rectangular card in half to make a square.

2. Open out the compass to 7cm wide.

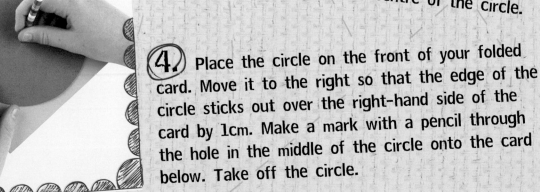

3. Draw a circle on the square piece of card and cut it out. Using the point of the compass, make a small hole in the centre of the circle.

4. Place the circle on the front of your folded card. Move it to the right so that the edge of the circle sticks out over the right-hand side of the card by 1cm. Make a mark with a pencil through the hole in the middle of the circle onto the card below. Take off the circle.

5. Close the compass up to 2cm wide and draw a circle on the folded card so that the edge of the circle is 2cm from the top and 2cm from the right-hand edge.

6. Cut out the circle.

7. Push the point of the paper fastener through the front of the folded card where you made the pencil mark (see step 4).

8. Push the point of the paper fastener through the middle of the circle of card. Open out the paper fastener.

9. Draw around the hole in the front of the card onto the wheel underneath. Move the wheel around until you cannot see the pencil lines. Draw around the hole again. Keep moving the wheel and drawing around the hole in the front until you have used up all the space on the wheel.

10. Take the paper fastener out of the card. Put a photo or picture under the cut-out circle on the front of the card and draw around it. Cut it out. Cut out as many photos and pictures as you have circles on the wheel. Stick the photos and pictures onto the circles on the wheel.

11. Put the card back together with the paper fastener. Decorate the front of the card. Turn the wheel to display your pictures.

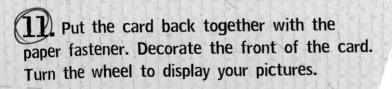

Origami card

You will need
- piece of coloured origami paper, or other coloured paper, 12.5cm x 15cm
- piece of coloured card, 21cm x 15cm
- scraps of shiny blue and yellow paper
- pair of scissors · glue · paintbrush · pen

Origami is the Japanese art of paper folding. 'Ori' means folding and 'kami' means paper in Japanese. Follow the steps below to make an origami boat to go inside a card.

1. Fold the piece of origami paper in half along the longest side. Fold the top corner of the folded side into the middle of the bottom edge like a triangle. Leave a border at the bottom.

2. Do the same with the top corner on the opposite side, making sure that the edges meet exactly.

3. Fold the bottom edge of the paper upwards.

4. Turn it over and do the same on the other side.

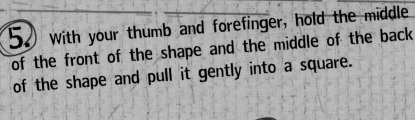

5. With your thumb and forefinger, hold the middle of the front of the shape and the middle of the back of the shape and pull it gently into a square.

6. Press the shape flat.

7. Take one of the bottom corners of the square and fold it upwards. Turn over the paper and fold the other corner in the same way. You now have a folded triangle.

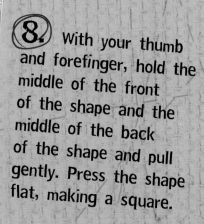

8. With your thumb and forefinger, hold the middle of the front of the shape and the middle of the back of the shape and pull gently. Press the shape flat, making a square.

9. Fold the coloured card in half, making a firm crease. Cut out wave shapes from the shiny blue paper and a yellow circle for the Sun. Glue these onto the inside of your card. Write your message.

10. Gently pull the outer corners of the square, to unfold your boat. Paint a thin line of glue along the length of the bottom of the boat. Stick the shape onto the inside of the card. Fold the shape flat. The person you give the card to can unfold the boat and float it on the sea.

HAPPY FATHERS DAY!

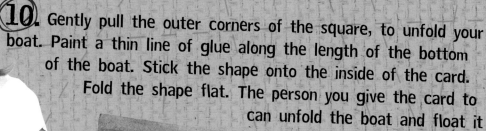

Origami

The art of origami is to make objects, such as animals, birds and flowers, by folding a single piece of paper. It is possible to make very intricate designs in this way. Some designs even have moving parts, such as birds with wings that flap.

119

Glowing card

Today's greetings cards come in all shapes and sizes. Some cards make noises, play music or light up when you open them. Follow these instructions to make a card in the shape of a tree with a glowing light at the top.

You will need

- piece of stiff card 22cm x 4cm
- ruler · pencil · sticky tape
- piece of paper 10cm x 17cm
- piece of stiff card 10cm x 17cm
- pair of scissors
- piece of green paper 10cm x 17cm
- glue · small bulb in a bulb holder
- small pieces of coloured paper
- 2 connectors with crocodile clip ends
- battery in a battery holder

1. To make a stand for your tree, measure 8mm along the long piece of card and make a mark. Measure a further 3cm and make another mark. Do the same again.

2. Make a fold in the card at each mark and tape the ends to make a box shape.

3. Fold the paper in half and draw half a Christmas tree in a pot, on the folded edge. Cut out the shape and use it as a pattern.

4. Using the pattern draw a tree shape on stiff card. Cut it out. Do the same with the green paper. Stick the green paper onto the card.

5. Stick the box onto the back of the tree at the bottom. Make a hole near the top of the tree. The hole must be large enough for the bulb to fit into it.

6. Decorate the front of the tree with cut-out paper shapes. Cut a star shape for the top of the tree. Cut a hole in the middle of the star the same size as the hole in the card. Stick the star onto the card.

7. Attach the crocodile clips on one end of each connector to each side of the bulb holder. Push the bulb gently through the hole in the tree.

8. Attach the crocodile clips to the connectors on either side of the battery holder. The bulb will light up. Take off one clip.

Circuits

To make the bulb light up, the electric current has to be able to flow from the battery to the lightbulb and back to the battery again. This is called a circuit.

9. Put the battery inside the box at the back of the tree. Move the wires so you cannot see them from the front. Re-connect the last wire to light up the tree just before you give it away.

Season's Greetings

acrobatics
Jumping and balancing acts to entertain people.

afterlife
Life after death. The Ancient Egyptians believed that their soul carried on living after they died.

amplify
To amplify sounds is to make them stronger or louder. On a thumb piano, the soundbox amplifies the sound.

antennae
The feelers on the head of an insect.

attract
When objects are pulled towards each other. The opposite poles of a magnet attract one another.

Buddhists
People who follow the teachings or religious beliefs of Siddhartha Gautama.

carnivorous
Animals, such as lions, and plants, such as the Venus flytrap, that eat meat.

chanting
Saying or calling words out in a special rhythm. Some religions, such as Buddhism, use chanting as a way to pray.

chrysalis
The hard cover a caterpillar makes around itself before it turns into a butterfly.

commedia dell'arte
The Italian theatre that was popular in the 16th to 18th centuries. Many of the plays featured the same characters, for example, Pierrot the clown.

connector
A device for connecting one object to another.

crocodile clips
Long clips that when opened look like the mouth of a crocodile.

crops
Plants, such as wheat, rice and maize, that are grown for food.

cross-hatch
To shade with small crosses.

Cupid
The son of the goddess Venus. Cupid is often pictured on Valentine cards shooting a bow and arrow to help people fall in love.

digestive juices
The substances that soften and break down food, inside an animal or plant.

drumheads
The part of a drum that you beat against, often with your hand or a stick.

e-card
A card designed on a computer and sent to people by e-mail. Many people send e-cards because they save on postage and paper, which is cheaper and good for the environment.

electric current
The movement of electrical energy around an electric circuit.

endangered
When there are very few of a certain kind of animal left in the wild. For example, the rhinoceros and the tiger are both endangered.

extinct
When there are no more of a certain animal left anywhere in the world. For example, dinosaurs are extinct.

felt
A type of material that is made by pressing wool together and heating it with steam.

flamenco
A type of dance done mainly in Spain. Flamenco dancers use castanets to tap out the rhythm of their dance.

gills
The parts of a fish's body that it uses to breathe.

gourd
The hard skin of a fruit. The skin is hollowed out and dried to make musical instruments.

intricate
Something that has lots of different parts. For example intricate origami has a lot of folds.

jester
A professional clown or joker. Jesters often wore pointy hats with bells on the end.

keyboard instruments
Musical instruments that have levers, pedals and keys that are pushed or pressed to create a note. Pianos and organs are keyboard instruments.

Latin America
Parts of Central and South America where Spanish and Portuguese are the main languages spoken.

Lent
The time from Ash Wednesday to Holy Saturday (the day before Easter). For Christians, Lent is a time for fasting (giving up certain foods) and prayer.

magnetic field
An invisible force that can attract or repel other objects or magnets.

masked ball
A dance where everyone wears a mask to cover some part or all of their face.

mass-produced
To produce or manufacture goods in large quantities, especially by machinery.

meditating
To meditate is to think deeply and seriously about something. Some religions use meditation as a type of prayer.

mummify
To treat a body with oils and wrap it in cloth to preserve it once it has been buried.

mummy
A body that has been wrapped in oils and bandages to preserve it or stop it from decaying.

origami
The traditional Japanese art of folding paper into animal or flower shapes.

papier mâché
Paper that has been made into a pulp or layered with a glue and water mixture to make objects that are solid when dry.

shilling
A type of coin that was used in Britain. It was equal to five pence.

soundbox
The hollow part of a string instrument that amplifies the sound, making it louder or stronger.

spoiler
A device used on racing cars to break up the air around them as they move. This helps to keep the car under control.

symmetrical
An exact reflection of a structure or pattern on either side of a dividing line.

wind instruments
Musical instruments that are blown or sucked to make a sound. Flutes and recorders are wind instruments.

Index